VOICES FROM THE PEN

VOICES FROM THE PEN

Edited by
MARK MAGEE

BOOK MARK PUBLICATIONS
61 Chingford Road Walthamstow London E17 4PW

Date of Publication
June 1998

Published in the UK by
Book Mark Publications
61 Chingford Road
Walthamstow
London E17 4PW

Telephone 0181 923 6183

Printed by:
ProPrint
Riverside Cottage
Great North Road
Stibbington
Peterborough PE8 6LR

ISBN: 1 902028 01 5

CONTENTS

HAINAULT FOREST

Sunlight shines through hazy sky,
Valley slips into green.
Trees and grasses before your eye,
Autumn turns a colourful scene.

A breathing space of Greater London,
People come from all around.
Peaceful hilltop, till sun down
Children, mums and dads abound.

In paddock animals grazing,
Bulls and lamas, spotted a sheep
Soon to return home, and sleep.

Fresh air, many people strolling,
Pleasant walks and sloping hills.
In distance, church bell tolling,
Relax, forget awhile the bills.

By the lake rippling waters
Glinting in the evening sun.
Fishermen, children and rail porters,
Sit patiently waiting, having fun.

Evening cricket on the plains,
Oh! Well caught, how's that!
Men and boys football playing,
Excitedly shouting 'give to Pat.'

Now the sun is setting low
High rise flats into view,
Car is turning towards Bow;
Noise, dogs, houses, back to you.

John Ainsley

THE SPEED OF LIGHT

Cats are funny, cats are sweet,
They drink their milk and eat their meat,
They'll chase a ball or bit of string,
They sit on fences where they sing,
They eat your plants and claw your chair,
They smile at you like they don't care,
They'll come in all wet and muddy,
After a fight with their buddy,
And sit on clean laundry or beds,
And get such pleasure when you turn red.
They chase the mice, the birds, their toys,
And chase a train set like little boys.
But most of all they're great to hold,
They warm you up when you are cold,
They cheer you up when you are sad
And soon you're playing with them, feeling glad.
You can't help but love them even if they bite
And do you know, cats have the speed of.....
LIGHT!

Caroline Allen

AT THE GRANDSLAM BALL

At last our minds are tuned as one
The game we play is not just for fun.
Your opening bid had me in a trance,
As you led me at the Friday dance.
I was nonetheless delighted at your inviting call,
My Friday Night Love, at the Grandslam Ball.

Your best 'ones' bade me a romantic incline;
My move in response, I was sure, would you entwine?
For I opted to stop next, into our Gerber stake-out,
You immediately insisted a positive break-out!
I summoned the verve and sway for the heights,
My choice of seventh heaven, secured surely, for shared delights!

For you to mastermind a waltzing display,
In your possessive, passionate, and yet clinical way,.
You glistened in diamonds, looking positively grand,
The entire club at your mercy, in the palm of your hand.
My royal heart was disposed as tender to treasure,
For my Friday Night Love, 'twas our Grandslam nights pleasure!

Ron Amato

CELEBRATION

Religion can be, by its nature, a very serious subject
And for most of us something we should not reject,
But there is a lighter side that many religions enjoy
Even some of the non believers are happy to join in the ploy,
One could almost call it a fancy dress ball
However in truth it is called a religious festival.

To have a celebration of this kind
Brings colour and happiness to mind,
For as we see such skill in costume made by many hands
And music played in various guises with many bands,
You are drawn in to join the celebration
And appreciate the work of art with admiration.

Other festivals revolve round fasting and food
The type of celebration to be approached in good mood,
For at the end of a period of self sacrifice and remembrance
There are certain things to eat before vast indulgence,
Then as you should with all new beginnings
Share in all the experiences with happy feelings.

We do well to appreciate the festive spirit
Which normally follows a period of far less credit,
For new beginnings are all part of creation
The new born, new years, months and seasons bring gratification
Above all a new birth within
So that your own new life can begin.

Ralph Andrews

DAYS GONE BY

Summers come and summers go
Time seems to go so fast,
Before we even know it
Childhood days have past.

Was it like this long ago
In the pleasant days of pleasure,
Nothing seemed to worry us
Life was full of leisure.

Perhaps it only felt like this
When we were in our prime,
Just enjoying what we had
We noticed not the time.

Why is that sometimes
Life becomes a bore?
Now we are always counting hours
Wondering what it all is for.

Barbara Appèl

TRIVIAL PURSUIT

Under cover of darkness, a mother searches for food,
Anything she can find, to satisfy her brood.
Furtively rummaging, for anything she can find,
Careful not to leave the best bits behind.

Back home, tucked up for the night safe and warm,
Two babies sleep soundly, unaware of any harm.
Mum carries out her wearisome task, until the break of dawn,
Then freezes in terror, as she hears a huntsman's horn.

Clumsy in her panic, she runs wildly in fright,
The huntsmen whoop gleefully in their delight.
Mum takes to her heels, at a furious pace,
Baffled at the looks of joy, on the huntsmen's face.

Hounds howling and barking,
Galloping horses,
And those unmistakable jackets of red.
This mother fox knows, she will soon be dead.

Back in the lair, two cubs awake, scared and hungry now,
They sense that something has happened to their mother somehow.
So outside they venture, for the first time, to the hounds delight,
And everyone ignores their piteous screams in the night.

Maureen Arnold

SOLO

Walking down a country lane,
With thoughts racing round my brain,
Why does time go so fast?
Why doesn't happiness last?

Looking at my old dog, once a mischievous pup,
Also at my children, all too soon grown up,
Living with their partners wanting to be on their own,
Not thinking how it feels to be all alone.

Another day over, find a book to take to bed,
There's no one here to talk to any more, so there's nothing to be said,
No one to say night, night, God bless, I love you.
Nobody here to notice if I am feeling blue.

A new day, and it's a beautiful morning, so we will go for a walk,
My old dog and me, just up the road, and along by the river lea,
And as I am walking, I am thinking of you my dear,
And wishing with all my heart, that you were still here.

Maureen Arnold

A FRIEND

A friend in him, a friend in me
Our lives they live as one,
The day I said 'I do to him'
The day I bore his son.

We tackle life with open arms
We guide each other through,
The ups the downs the circles
How much I care for you.

Imagine your the ocean
I'd ride the waves as one,
For never just a husband
But the earth, the moon, the sun.

A friend and yet a little more
For me your always there,
We have the next eternity
And more to always share.

Dawn Avery

A ROCK AT SEA

To think a thousand thoughts a day
Of worries wills and woes.
To dream along a dawdled way
Or flare in furied anger throes.

To mark the memory of a stolen kiss
With the sense of a scented smile.
To gaze into space in glazed-eyed bliss
Or feel far away for a while.

To hiss and split in heated hatred.
To condemn. To curse. To crack
To swear such vows of solemn revenge.
To shun forever and never look back.

With feelings so flippant as stormy weather,
With moods so many between pain and pleasure,
Smiles and tears and words that shock,
Thank you, my Lord, thou art my rock.

Alison Awcock

THE FIRE'S GOLDEN LIGHT

Whispered words of love fall, from his sweet lips
Darkness cloaks the room, as hands rest on hips
I feel a rain of kisses, fall upon my face,
As we are locked as one, in an everlasting embrace.

The ticking seems to stop, from the clock upon the wall
As in a fatal love, unknowingly I start to fall,
As I look into his face, I see his soul beneath his eyes
But the light of my love, hides the pack of lies.

We start to move together, in the rhythm lovers know,
As we bask in the warmth, from the fire's golden glow.
I touch his face and hair, as if to prove that he is real
As it is like a dream that it is him that I feel.

To the peak of ecstasy, we glide as one soul and heart,
As words of love pour from his lips, swift to impart.
As the feeling hits, we float upon a cloud,
Dropping the rules of earth, like an unwanted shroud.

When our passion is spent, I lay across his skin
Feeling the heat of our love, the joy starts seeping in
He looks into my eyes, and softly strokes my hair,
I have found my soul-mate in our lovers lair.

He begins to move, fear clutches my soul,
My happiness is leaving, into the desolate black hole,
He turns and tells me, that he has to leave tonight
And he will always remember me in the fire's golden light.

Janine Ayres

SPRING BUTTERFLY

Life is as a spring butterfly
Yesterday resting, weak
Today happy, basking, in the sun.
Tomorrow soaring high,
Beyond is autumn alone
Finally fading before the winter snow.

Is life as a spring butterfly?
Or is life only a step towards death:
The death of our world,
Death by pollution
Death by a greedy few:
Whose greed is wiping out tomorrow's world.

Yesterday's rain forests, turned by
today's greed into desert wastes:
By people greedy for their timber.
Mining for oil, gas, minerals and gems,
Turning everything into a barren desert
A land of tears for Tomorrow's people.

Teeming fish dying in polluted rivers and seas:
Dead - unfit to be eaten,
Unfit for human, unfit for seabird, seal or bear,
A death sentence for all:
Pollution
Fumes in the air - killing all!
So must we all fade before the winter snow?
Fading as surely as a Spring Butterfly.

Doreen Banas

'THE PASSING YEARS'

Fine white horses galloping by,
Through the valley of the sky.
Years are passing, quickly passing,
But the valley's everlasting.

Too many years of travel - alone,
Years of silence, without a moan.
Violence, beatings, hatred too,
Enduring with hope, the long-range view.

Lonely as a desert breeze,
Blowing through the desert trees.
Breaking on a lonely shore,
Knocking on a special door.

'Open up, Dear God,' a cry at last,
'Will this pain, this life-never pass?'
The Angel of Death is hovering near,
A welcome end it would appear.

Passing now, by all unseen,
All forgiven; slate wiped clean.
Take these ashes, toss out to sea,
Thus may travel - for eternity.

Years are passing, quickly passing,
For the valley's everlasting.
Fine white horses galloping by,
Through the valley of the sky.

Doreen Banas

WHAT IS IT?

What is love I would love to know
Does it get bigger, does it grow.
Do some have more than others to give,
Is it something we are born with?

Is love when he walks through the door
And drops his bag and coat on the floor,
Or brings you his clothes with so much sorrow
And asks you sweetly will they be ready tomorrow?

Is love the arguments shouting and tears,
Or afterwards when comes all the sneers
Do you wish all the time they would walk away,
But be sure they came back another day?

Is love just a smile or a nod of his head,
Or if he gave you a cuddle instead?
He didn't bring flowers, chocolates or wine
But that will save for another time.

Is love all the words he never says
But tries to show you in other ways?
The gentle touch of a warming hand,
That makes you feel so soft and grand.

I think that love is all of these,
Loves little droplets carried on a gentle breeze.
The good and the bad, it's all the same
I suppose that's why it brings so much pain

Tracey Barrett

THE ZOO

We who live inside this zoo,
Watch the destruction humans do.
Vandalised parks, broken trees,
See pollution of the seas.
Fish that die, birds can't fly,
And Seals, we ask the reason why,
These gentle creatures have to die,
To make the coats vain women buy.
Why can't the Whale enjoy the sea,
The Elephant keep his ivory,
Why must Deer and Foxes run,
Rabbits tremble at the gun.
Gentle Badgers in terror wait,
The agony of the Badger bait.
Bright coloured Parrots soared their domain,
In forests where gently fell the rain.
A thing of beauty to behold,
Homeless now, out in the cold.
Tropical forests all have gone,
Destruction going on and on.
Beaver, Mink, Ocelot,
Becomes a coat some humans got.
The Tiger and Polar Bear can't roar,
For they're a mat on someone's floor.
The powerful Rhino, too must fall,
His feet for a stand in someone's hall.
The King of the jungle lost his head,
To adorn a fireplace instead.
If only our ways they would heed,
We only kill for the food we need.
It was never part of God's great plan,
To subject us to the greed of man.

Yet, invading our world, you will find them,
Letting pride and envy blind them.
We see the point of having bars,
But who should be behind them?

Irene Beattie

NO STING

Once we lived our lives side by side
Inhabiting the same world.
Now you have moved on.
My world is laughter and tears,
Both joys and pains.
The struggle of our physical nature.
You left that behind.
Your world is full of peace.
You know a depth of love.
Beyond my understanding.
Pain, hunger, fear and loneliness,
All this is behind you now.
We co-exist in separate planes
Connected only by memories,
My world such a poor image of yours,
Some part of you still lives in mine.
One day I shall live in yours.
There is no goodbye.
We are living apart until we meet again.

Ros Beeswing

'HELP THROUGH CRISES'

Hearts have been broken,
Only Christ, can mend,
For He has spoken -
Wants crises to end!

He offers His arm
To lift and support
While nerves He does calm -
Sends Love beyond thought!

He comes to rescue
Those to Him, do turn.
He keeps promise, too -
Says Words we should learn!

Each Word we must keep
(Since, His Love does show)
In our hearts so deep -
That makes them all glow!

Patricia Bolton

MIRACLE

The power of the light,
It burns deep in my soul,
The strength that it has given me,
Has filled the gaping hole.

I feel I am one again,
Free from all that binds,
I feel I could do anything
Defy all space and time.

Something must have saved me,
I thought my time had come,
Looking down from high above
Everything and everyone.

I saw myself just laying there,
People huddled round,
The sirens getting closer,
As I bled there on the ground.

The further that I rose,
The less that I could see,
Surely this was all a dream,
It surely was not me.

It was then the miracle happened,
Everywhere became so bright,
I felt a warmth inside of me,
It must be from the light.

Then I woke in hospital,
At first it felt quite odd,
Now I describe my experience,
As the day I was touched by God.

Amanda Brind

'TOO LATE'

Friendship is like a garden,
If it is to flourish
It must be constantly tended.

Friendship came and sweetly blossomed,
Shedding forth her radiance,
But first neglected, then forgotten,
She didst <u>wither</u> and decay!

Too late, she cried pathetically,
Ere she completely passed away!
'If I'm to flourish, I must be
Tended always, constantly!'

Joan Carter

IMPORTANT THINGS THEY NEVER TEACH YOU IN SCHOOL

How to truly love someone,
How to be famous and rich,
How to end a relationship that's 'done,'
Or how to quieten regret's itch.

What to say to someone who is dying,
How to know what others are thinking really,
How to tell if someone is lying,
Or how to let go, someone you loved dearly.

How to accept things you can't help or change,
How to spend your life being poor,
How not to fear and hate the strange,
Or how to abide that ass the law.

These twelve things they never teach,
We must learn the hard way each.

Robert Cave

THE MASK OF SECRETS

Can you keep a secret?
It sounds such a simple task,
Your mind only on what you'll get
And never on the mask.

The mask, you can deny,
If at secrets you do balk,
Or you let your promise fly
When you or others wish to talk.

The mask, should you choose to wear it.
Hides your promise and your face,
And although it won't show it
The mask sets you apart from the human race.

The mask is a terrible burden
And isolation is it's task,
A burden that you cannot share, beholden,
It is the price of the mask.

Robert Cave

LES OISEAUX DE LISBONNE

Judges with sins more scarlet (maybe?) than red their robes
Fling life-mangled lives into a limbo of quite false existence
Though none doubt their beetle-brows and such pursed lips
As they turn to yet another catastrophe bound in bright ribbon.

The prisoners, pole-axed by providence - pale quickly
Pallid lives in pallid clothes with a pallid future.
Perforce to 'come to terms...', or to - 'accept the inevitable'
Unable now to do other then - 'fly by automatic pilot.'

Which is apposite since their flight-path now is a queue
Always queues. Queues for function - as in personal fate,
Like in queues for grey cell's constant incarcerating,
Or in queues for grey food's inevitable grey ingestion.

Grey shirts acquire a colour clouding memory into vapour
Grey skies scud past a far church steeple's familiar greyness
Visitors' forced chatter hides grey admission of hateful duty and,
Empty letters bring nothing but grey reminder of despair's identity

Prominently grey amongst all grey shades are the old, grey heads
Grey, old lives with slack, grey cheeks and blue, grey lips
Grey, old teeth gnashing grey, old feet paddling, grey, old guts slobbering
Wheezing old, grey sighs and sobs - sadly cobwebbed in a grey spittle

Grey cells, grey galleries of docketed grey lives - utter greyness
Only together as in some perpetual, grey, hypochondriac queue
Whispering of some grey, forlorn hope's last bid for ashen, winter Glory
Bleak-blown, splattered-out, wasted and then? Greyed to gravel!

Time slowly consumed in dreaming old man's unknowable fantasy
Unable to accept a young man's place and it's utterly cruel contempt
Dreading the daily assault on any residual, remaining, ebbing dignity
Harsh laughs draining life and drowning redemption - retreat into nullity

Grey prison hospitals' silence and antiseptic empty smell of Lifelessness
Grey last gasp denied a darling's last whisper of dearness and,
Grey-suited prison governor's grey hand of administrative sympathy
To die, O loving Lord? O yes! But first - spare us that.

Andrew Challen

A WHISPER IN THE FIELDS

Silence was the only sound
Before I opened my ears to listen,
But now there's light, almost mellow swooshing.
As the wind races to and fro.

I hear the sound of tweeting birds
As their wings flap within the clouds,
And crickets fiddling in the grass
Beneath trooping ants as they climb a settled bark.

Leaves rustling in trees up high
As the early signs of shower fall;
Tiny bombs of water exploding on a leaf,
Its crisp cracking echoing along the wind.

The more I listen, the more I hear,
'Till I can record sounds from afar:
A dog's low growl, an engine hum,
A whispering in the fields.

C.P. Clarke

SHROUDED IS THE NIGHT

Fog that hides the night, fog that hides the day,
Everything is white, you can't find your way.
Swirling around our face, swirling round and round,
I can't see my feet, it's reaching to the ground.

Closing in the old oil lamp with its flickering light,
I can feel my heart, beating with all its might.
I turn my head around, now ghostly shapes appear,
My mouth is dry, from the stifling fear.

There must be people near, for I can hear their feet,
Walking on the cobble stones echoing through the street.
I can hear the sound of horses hooves coming from somewhere,
I pull my shawl tight around me, covering my hair.

I must be by the churchyard, not looking left or right,
An owl hoots, but wait, is that a glimmer of a light?
It could be from the window of the cottage by the lane,
But how do I know? Nothing looks the same.

They say the old lady, who lives there is a witch,
My nerves are taut, I feel at screaming pitch.
A tall dark figure is standing over me,
I trip and fall, hitting hard my knee.

A voice calls out, a voice I know so well,
It's a voice I love, saying is that you our Sal?
Yes, yes it's me dad, I call out as best I can,
He lifts me up in his arms as gently as a lamb.

I'm carried up the path and through the cottage door,
Mums waiting for me by the fire, I'm not afraid any more.

Kathleen Coggins

NOT WHAT I CALL DEMOCRACY

The politicians are out in force
To gain a vote from us of course.
They visit each county with their cries
To give us promises and to f eed us lies.

Election day is not far away
It's our duty to vote, so they say.
The democratic process is nothing but a farce
They bicker and argue like kids in a class.

So why should we vote?
We've nothing to gain.
Whoever gets in
Will be just the same.

They tax us here,
They tax us there
They say it's lawful,
But it's so unfair.

They took us into Europe
Not giving us a choice,
They take just what they want from us,
Without listening to our voice.

They took away our rights from us,
Then prance around in their big flash bus,
Now they want a vote from you and me,
That's not what I call democracy.

Valerie Colbert

MODERN TIMES

People we see keep rushing around,
Watching the clocks, pounding the ground.
A quick 'halo; how are you today'
Catch you later, sorry can't stay.
People to see and places to go,
I remember when the pace of life was easy and slow.
There was a time, a long while ago, when
We would stand watching the world go by then.
How I wish those times would come again,
It's fast cars and faster planes, none of us can stand the strain.
Escape is what we need, escape is what we pray,
And I did that just yesterday.
Walking through fields, climbing over styles,
Passing silent streams, walking for miles.
I feel the sun warming my back,
Seeing the woods ahead, I'm making tracks.
A pungent smell is filling my head,
Decades of leaves forming a carpet on which to tread.
Reaching up to catch a shaft of sun shining through,
Watching rabbits, hearing the first cuckoo.
I'm going home now to the clatter and chatter
I escaped for awhile, so now it doesn't matter.

Brenda Coley

THE ROYAL DOCKS

Stillness and silence, has cloaked this once majestic scene,
These were the greatest docks at one time, the world had ever seen,
Ships from many countries that had been secured against these berths,
Arrived with their precious shipments, from over this mighty earth.

Powerful cranes swung into action, to unload their allotted charge,
And placement was made of these cargo's, into a floating barge,
The remaining freight was sorted, and allocated far and wide,
Some was transferred to other ships, before the ebbing tide.

Warehouses filled with merchandise, foods, wines and fancy hats,
Goods already chosen, had been loaded on to transport, ready for Dispatch,
Strong and steady men did the work, and accomplished it with such Pride,
But some workers did not stay long, others did, until they died.

The mighty docks were blasted, but not closed by the Kaiser's flying Men,
Hitler also attempted to destroy 'The Royal Docks' but simply failed Again,
Throughout those years the docks survived, and a tale can now be told,
The people that had worked here those years, were very brave and bold.

Within this complex, battles were fought, by men for their workers Rights,
When conditions asked for did not change, workers voted to go on Strike,
At last the changes did arrive, for the better off for the worse,
Some say it made them very happy, and others just cried and cursed.

The closure of this mighty dockland, was due to advancements and
Gain,
Containers are now the way of life, and easier dispatched by train,
Progress they say must go on, but days here, will not be the same,
The generation now living there, use that water just for sport and
Games.

To that past era where our forefathers, achieved their daily task,
I raise my hat and think of them, and a time that's completely past.

Roy Coppin

SNUBBED EARTH

What is happening to this world, that was so green and true,
they're chopping down the mighty forest, poisoning the sea once blue.
No longer do we breathe clean air, or bathe in waters without care,
Every day the tabloids print, stories and scenes that do us scare.

The ozone layer is getting thin, natures changed her methodical ways,
Birth by creatures is now earlier, and sometimes twice in 90 days,
Changing weather as times go by, temperatures go from low to high,
Has now turned this divine environment against us, and to slowly die.

The greed of man has changed life, that way, our ancestors knew,
Benefits that should be shared by all, is now for just a selfish few,
Man has spoiled this earth of treasures and leave an unfruitful void,
This is now a world of shame, it should be nursed, and just not toyed.

Roy Coppin

VIJAYA

A dashing figure slick black hair and Elvis Presley glasses
A mellow voice crooning into the old microphone -
You were the face of the Sixties for the SLBC's many phases
As you presented old favourites and releases,
To an adoring public.
You were the personality of the year
In Sri Lanka,
Rising from the ranks to lead the airwaves
In a radio revolution
You were a star and how you knew it -
They paid good money to see you
And hear your voice -
Then,
It happened -
The unexpected, the earth shattering,
The devastating news
Struck down with cancer -
A three month sentence
Hanging over your head.
But you said faith could move mountains
You were going to be healed -
By the stripes of Jesus.
They laughed, they pitied, they gossiped,
Even talking about the future of your children.
The President was stunned -
The island cried.
God moved -
And a miracle happened in London.

Complete healing
He turned your soul
Away from sin -
So that you
Could spread his message of love,
To a needy nation.

Ivan Corea

(This poem is dedicated to Dr Vijaya Corea,
former Director-General of the SLBC now a leading Evangelist)

GRANDY

Gentle soul
I remember you so vividly
In my mind's eye
You loved God and your fellowmen
How we adored you
Priest, grandfather, friend.
You sang lullabies, Clementine
Was lost every night
So that we could rest easy,
Underneath a star struck
Colombo sky
In sleepy Maha Nuge Gardens
The lane was quiet
As you sang softly to your grandchildren
You encouraged us to know about God
And experience His Son's Love.
A trip to the corner book-shop to buy a book or a picture,
Comics from the book man who cycled in every month with his
Selection
Were special treats.
One day father sat us down, he broke the news
You had gone away for good
A screaming ambulance flew down the Madampe-Colombo run,
It was all in vain
When you died our little hearts were shattered
We could not hear you or feel your love,
We miss you, kind soul, dear Grandy.

Ivan Corea

(This poem is dedicated to the late Rev. Canon Ivan Corea.
Former Vicar of St. Luke's Church, Borella, Sri Lanka)

LONG SUFFERING MOTHER

Childhood brings back so many memories
And how I remember
Your endless trips
To Colombo's markets, bread queues at Perera & Sons,
Visits to the Kollupitiya Co-op with the ration book in hand,
A sweet at Marikar Brothers, clothes at Mangarems,
A book from Lake House.
You trudged the streets
In the hot sun -
To buy us food
You suffered the insults of rude traders in the boutiques,
When credit was closed,
But you pleaded on our behalf.
I did not realise
You sold your gold bangles
To pay for our education.
Your love for us was limitless
You went that extra mile.
How you have suffered
And still do
Despite the rocky road, the thorns
And the heartache
Your heart is full of love
For your kith and kin,
The grandchildren,
Your friends and the church.
You radiate the love of Jesus -
I need to stop
And thank you
For what you have done for us
Dearest Mother.

Ivan Corea

ACHCHI - UNDYING GRATITUDE

Time changes feelings they say
Growing up in Colombo
You saw us as troublesome grandchildren
But you stayed
When I was vulnerable, you took me to school
Waiting for hours under the shade of a tree,
You brought my lunch with you.
We teased you as you sat under the Jam tree
In Maha Nuge Gardens in your cane red chair
Reading your horoscope and the Sinhla papers
Wake up time was 5.30 a.m. every morning
Preparing our meals for the day
But you started with a prayer
Communication time with our Lord,
As regular as clockwork
You spoke to him
On a direct link
But we failed to understand.
You loved Christ and was close to him,
Even when your sight failed you
And they left you in a darkened room.
Your confusion was touching
35,000 feet on an aircraft, eating a bread roll with butter
You thought you were on a train
Not feeling the stress of a pressurised cabin.
You always said Thank you,
When we fetched water.
You blessed us but we had to be grateful to you,
For all that you did for us
One morning the Lord took you away
After days in a hospital
We wept
We had lost a part of our heart.

Ivan Corea

FATHER TO SON - TO CHARIN

Every morning
You have a puzzled look.

You see me go
And your eyes are sad.

As I depart,
Your hug is full of love.

When I return
You greet me like a long lost friend.

Ah, you cry, welcome home
And your smile says it all.

You are a bundle of energy
Laughter and tears.

I pray that you will stay close
To God in the coming years.

One day you might well open the door
To your heart and let Jesus in.

Beware of the wolves, avoid materialism
And turn away from sin.

Seek peace, joy
And happiness in a transitory life.

LOVE GOD
And love your fellowmen.

Ivan Corea

WHAT IF....

Shall I be a nightingale
And sing my song to thee?
For in the beauty of the night
I sing it tenderly.

If I was a wandering bird
I would take my leave
And wait until the spring returned
Eager to receive

Your faithful trust and loving care
Your smiles, your watching eye,
Your face not sad, but only fair
And together we would fly.

To north and south and west and east
to countries rare and old
We'd chat until the night had ceased
Till nothing was untold.

Then we would rest until the ray
Of light would waken us from sleep
And we'd welcome yet another day
To loiter and to leap

Into the future of the morn
Where everything in us was born.

Margrit Dahm

THE SEAGULLS

Down at the shipyard by the sea
I stood and watched them fly and suddenly
In a charade they came swiftly passing by.

They sensed my presence and pretended
Not to see me in my height and defended
In lines of crescents what to them seemed only right.

So we stood and watched each other at the shipyard
By the sea they the guard and me the bother -
It could have gone on endlessly,

But then a stir was in the air,
They took off gracefully and released me
As it were from my winged captivity.

Margrit Dahm

YOU

Your heart beat fast.
Your eyes were closed tight.
You held me closely...
Through the long cold night.

I had cried all night long,
But you were there for me,
With your loving smell,
The way I like you to be.

I slept in your arms,
You held me with care.
I knew I was safe now,
As you softly played with my hair.

Your hand skimmed lightly,
Over my tearful face.
Your lips met mine,
And I felt your warm taste.

You then told me you loved me,
And I knew it was true.
You'd always be there for me,
No matter what I'd do.

Gemma Davis

INSIDE

I scream in my sleep,
I cry in my wake.
As the nightmare still haunts me,
I just wish it was all fake.

I am alone,
And everyday I'm scared.
I want someone there,
So my problems can be shared.

I try and be happy,
And put on a brave face.
But deep inside it hurts,
As in my mind it's a chase.

The feelings won't ever go,
You'll always be in my mind
Now I must try to carry on,
The rest of my life I must find.

I'll never forget it though,
The pain you put me through.
I must get you out of my thoughts,
It's something I don't know how to do.

There'll be many nights of crying,
And talking alone to myself.
But I'm determined to carry on,
And not be left alone on a shelf.

Gemma Davis

MY LOVE

Too late to stop the railway train taking my love away,
Wheels repeating angry words I never meant to say!

Sad and weary, sore at heart, my footsteps heavy and slow,
Aimlessly wandering from place to place, not caring where I go!

I stumble over stones and steps and walk thro' puddles and streams,
Tasting disillusionment of all my hopes and dreams.

The dark grey clouds reflect my mood of utter deep despair.
Then thro' the veil of mist and rain I see **you** standing there!

Suddenly the sun bursts thro' and a rainbow arcs the sky,
I gaze upon your smiling face and know the reason why.

My senses stir and my feet grow wings as the sky turns blue and gold!
Then in my arms I hold you tight with thankfulness untold.

The misery melted in my heart and sang like a bird set free,
The world became a **wonderful** place, for my love had returned to me!

Kathy Davis

THE MOUNTAIN

Climb the mountain oh so high,
And see if you can touch the sky,
Standing in the valley below,
It doesn't seem so far to go.

Climb it on a lovely day,
And try hard not to lose the way,
Do not go off on your own,
Keep away from the unknown.

Climb the mountain oh so tall,
Watch your step and do not fall,
When you finally reach the top,
Be prepared for your ears to 'pop.'

Climb down safely once you've seen,
The beautiful view of where you've been,
Tell your friends so they can try,
To climb the mountain oh so high.

Marion Denmark

A STORY TOLD

The pen was sent gliding
Across the clean, crisp page,
Words slowly formed
A sentence, a paragraph written.

A pencil drew lines
Formed shapes of all sizes
The colours added
A picture completed.

Words now written,
Pictures drawn
The cover added
A story told.

Claire C Dobson

FAR AWAY DREAMS

I sit beneath the sunshade
The sun warm upon my skin.
And close my eyes and dream once more
Of the places I have seen.

I hear the sound of aircraft
Drawing lines upon the sky,
And recall the far off places
Fresh and safely stored in my mind.

Full of Eastern Promise
The desert stole my heart,
The memories I keep with me
Will never fade or part.

These places that I once did see
Remain a part of me,
And when I'm feeling down and low
My dreams take me where I long to be.

Because although these thoughts are old
I sometimes wish to try,
To bring back all my yesterdays
My dreams of days gone by.

Tracy Earey

AIR BALLOON

Travelling down the motorway
It's true you see some sights.
Whilst sitting in that lorry cab,
I witnessed that maiden flight.

At first I caught them in my view
I wondered what they were,
But as they travelled closer,
I felt my insides stir.

It wasn't just a flock of birds
Or an aeroplane or two,
But a magical array of balloons,
That made my heart go phew!

It may sound a bit silly
Or maybe even daft,
But never before have I witnessed,
Such a beautiful, relaxing craft.

They came, I saw, they passed
Into the distance out of sight,
Forever in my memory,
The magical air balloon maiden flight.

Tracy Earey

FROM EGG TO AIR

So like a bird from egg to air
Came creation everywhere
Came forth a newer day
A memory made one might say.

So like a flower from bulb to bloom
Come the vastness of an empty room
Came the light of wisdom's eye
A petals climb from earth to sky.

So like a dream from mind to matter
Came a blind dreary chatter
Came the pace that sets our form
A trip from real that consumes the norm.

So like a man from ape to God
Came destruction with a nod
Came the end of humanity's rule
Another animal rise and fall.

Tony Eke

A LOVING ROSE

And in a world so full of roses
All of which are sadly torn
Lies alone one so proud
The rose most tall I say aloud
And in that rose so proud so tall
Hides more beauty than them all
So again aloud I will shout
That this rose will know no doubt
But take away that roses form
And apparent becomes the roses scorn
For tucked away within beauties eye
Are the deceiving thorns of natures lie.

Tony Eke

THE VALLEYS FAIR

River Wye travelling a picturesque path,
Swan with cygnets, duck with ducklings,
View creating a tranquil aftermath.

Canoeists in dazzling colourful activity,
Havocing the river's natural flow,
Additional movement amongst the rapids,
Gleaming river beneath sun's glow.

Cruiser gliding slowly along the river,
Bedecked in blooms of every myriad hue,
In sight, vestige of a railway route,
View recalled as a train passed through.

Area of outstanding natural beauty,
Down to river, sweeping carpet of trees;
Golden Valley; borders of England and Wales,
Scenery to move as far as the human eye sees.

Lesley Eldred

LOVE'S WAY

How can I show that I love you?
By letting you take me to dine,
Let you pursue and court me,
Let your heart and mine entwine.

How can I show that I love you?
By letting you enter my life,
Let you fill it with pleasure,
Permit you to be my wife.

How can I show that I love you?
By letting you nourish my frame,
Let you care for and tend me,
Be my crutch if I go lame.

How can I show that I love you?
By letting you suckle my heirs,
Help me nurture and mould them,
And answer all their prayers.

How can I show that I love you?
By letting you sit by my side,
Know my thoughts without speaking,
Contented and filled with pride.

How can I show that I love you?
By beside me letting you learn,
How to show that you love me,
Doing the same in return.

Charles Elsey

FOR THE ONE I LOVE

You came into my life
Before I was old enough to love you.
You left before I learnt how to tell you.
Today I stand for your belief in me,
For I know where ever you are,
You are still watching over me.

You gave me faith
Teaching me to look at myself.
Learning not to run,
From what I saw; scared me.

Your eyes knew how to look deep,
Deep into my soul.
With every glance
Healing the pain.

Touching my heart, was your goal,
Wiping away my tears
You showed me my soul.

As you sat watching me grow
You taught me what I didn't know
You showed me every possibility,
Opened my eyes to all I now know.

Honest
Strong and intelligent
You leave me today,
No longer the scarred little girl
You once found on a rainy day.

But I wonder if you are proud,
As you look down
At what you see
Now you know this is really me.

Z.H

EVERYTHING I WANT TO BE

Why do you smile at me with your eyes?
While I look at you with envy.

Why do you stand with life and purity?
Whilst I stand with death and indecency.

Why do you walk with your head up so high
Looking down on me with your rosy eyes?

Why do you look so superior and real?
Whilst I look so inferior and false.

But, yet why are you everything I want to be?

Z.H

THE ARTIST

Music dips and swells, as I my brush in hand,
See once more my Yorkshire, from crag, to sea and land,
Of harvesting the ploughman steers, his tractor busy still,
Please, my father, take me home, to my cot up on the hill.

Away from loneliness and fear, direct me 'ere I stray,
My body alone doth dwell herein, my soul be miles away,
Please take me to my hills and dales, my sea, my castles strong,
Though loved ones be not far away, I've been away too long.

Jonathan Field

FIRST CRY

Child of love, so newly born,
Your cry doth touch my tears,
Be not afraid, oh little one,
Love shall dispel your fears.

The threshold waits to watch you grow,
With courage, faith and love,
And from the Heavens shall come to you,
A gliding snow white dove.

He'll lead you to the straightest path,
Hope shall be your guide,
But if you call, I'll comfort thee,
And we'll walk, side by side.

Jonathan Field

SECOND THOUGHTS

Things are bad and that's no joke
I've paid the bills and now I'm broke.
Can't start the car, started to rain,
I've dropped my doorkey down the drain.
My wife's asleep in bed with flu,
I can't get in what can I do?

An open window, I climb in
I knock the vase it starts to spin,
The vase that I displayed with pride,
Given to me when my Nan died,
It topples falls then hits the floor
That nice old vase is a vase no more.

Remember as I clear the bits,
My Nan's stories of the blitz
V.1's bombs incendiaries
Delivered by our enemies.
Home wrecked twice by fire and blast
Lost all her treasures from the past.

Piercing wailing hellish sound
Buildings crushing to the ground.
Women screaming, children dying
Grown men wandering dazed and crying,
Bodies lying torn apart
Sights that would break my heart.

It makes me think, it makes me mad,
Why should I think that things are bad
I should give thanks for all I've got,
For what I have is quite a lot.
And my Nan's tales of folk's despair,
I'm really glad I wasn't there.

Bruce Fisher

CHILD OF THE UNIVERSE

You are a child of the universe
Disregarding colour or creed,
You have a right to our respect
You also feel and need.

The need to be accepted
The right to speak one's mind,
To express your inner feelings,
You should not be denied.

The entitlement of equality
In a modern world like ours,
Old ideas must be abolished,
You should not stand and cower.

Why should you not be suited
To an education as good as mine,
To enable you to succeed in life,
And excel in jobs as fine.

If we accepted people
Just for what they are,
Perhaps world-wide disputes could be resolved
And violations not occur.

You a child of the universe
Be proud.
Live, life.

Lynda Fordham

V.E. DAY

It's V.E. Day and all these years
Since England won the war.
And there became peace in our land,
Not hatred our country bore.
Just take a minute, sit and think,
Of all lives that were lost.
For freedom in our Country....
Death was what it cost.
Keep a solemn two minutes for you all,
That were England's public past,
May today we all salute to you,
For the victory that you cast.

Kelly J. Francis

THE WORLD WILL KNOW MY NAME

The boy walked down the country lane,
Once more at peace as nature healed his pain,
His gentle face both captured and beguiled,
But only turned his cruel father wild.

His hair was tangled, hanging in a mass,
His ragged clothes depriving him of class.
As he walked, he dreamed of love and fame,
One day, he thought, **the world will know my name**.

With courage, and with hope, he would survive,
At least his dreams would help him stay alive
He turned, prepared to play his role,
To face the years before he reached his goal.

Valerie Gamble

THE LONELY CLOWN

He wiped the heavy make-up from his face,
His weary eyes gazed through the mirror into space,
His wife, his only love, had died,
The lonely clown bowed his head and cried.

From his performance the audience couldn't guess,
That behind the humour there was deep distress,
For 30 years she had nestled by his side,
The lonely clown bowed his head and cried.

She had begged him not to let the circus down,
So many children loved to see him clown,
All he wanted at this moment was to hide,
The lonely clown bowed his head and cried.

She had been so brave and never once complained,
Even though, with pain, her face was lined and strained,
But remembering his promise as he'd held her like a child,
The lonely clown slowly raised his head and smiled.

Valerie Gamble

THE PAGES OF TIME

Now to turn the pages in rhyme,
And travel to London way back in time,
To late 18th century my journey goes,
When elegant ladies for Gainsborough did pose.

These ladies wore beautiful long flowing dresses,
With hair arranged into curly tresses,
A delightful picture to capture the eye
Of any gentleman passing by.

No buses or cars with polluting forces,
Just the noisy clatter of carriages and horses,
Wending their way through dimly lit streets,
A brief glimpse of dark shapes filling the seats.

The dandies in their silken hose,
A hanky tied up to delicate nose,
Wore velvet jackets in colours so fine,
And wigs with tailpieces tied behind.

The gentlemen had such style and grace,
Wearing elegant shirts with cuffs of lace,
How exciting they were to see,
Bowing low romantically.

Coming back to the present day,
I am grateful for the easier way
That we can enjoy our lives,
But it's nice to look back on olden times.

Valerie Gamble

SINK OR SWIM

What hurts me the most,
What I find so cruel,
Are those tankers at sea
Who are transporting fuel.

In the wake of the storm
They are battered and tossed,
Shaken and splintered
Like a floating match-box.

Out of them spews
This revolting black muck
Which attacks, when let loose,
Seagull, swan or duck.

It gushes out forth
Into the rough sea,
And attacks all it finds
Like a vile enemy.

A slimy trail spreads
Onto all it reaches,
And leaves it's black scum
Over rocks and beaches.

You may have all heard
Of the monsters at sea,
But this is what I think
The **Worst** monstrosity!!!

Anne Green

SPRING

Rows of tall bare trees
Standing in mid-autumn spree,
So lifeless and without thrill
As if nature had come to stand still.

No sound of fluttering wings
Or the sound of chirping birds
Only a sea of silence,
Heard.

As nature lies still
Waiting for the spring
Longing to hear a melody,
A cuckoo bird sing.

At last, branches new leaves have borne,
Branches with shoots of new life adorn,
Now spring is here in full bloom
Gone are the days of autumn gloom.

Aruna Hamid

COTTAGE ROMANCE

I used to dream I was so lazy, living in those summer days.
I use to scheme some say I was crazy, as I lived in that summer haze.
I visualised a country cottage, in a quaint old village street,
Like the ones that adorn chocolate boxes, all lovingly what a treat.
I could smell the country perfume, laden on the breeze,
As I lay down upon the softest of grass, gazing up at the trees.

All this I visualised, in my home town of dirt and grime,
What a perfect paradise I wish oh, how I wish it could be mine.
Dreaming still I kept that cottage, it had roses entwined around the door,
A little seat inside the porch, who could ask for more?
That treasured little abode was kept so trim and neat,
With chintz curtains at its windows and I'd wave to all to greet.

The garden was a picture, as I wandered amongst the flowers,
All waiting in that garden as they were drenched with passing showers.
You appeared my love so radiant, like that of the morning blue,
Could you not imagine us together in that cottage made for two.
Your eyes shone with gladness, as we wandered hand in hand,
In that beautiful part of England where no grime or dirt abounds.

Some day when fate permits, and wishes do come true,
My dreams will be realised and we shall return anew,
To that dearest little cottage, in that quaint old village street,
And we will gossip with our country neighbours and wave to all we greet.
Back to this reality amongst the dirt and grime I dream,
If only I cold persuade the hand of fate to help this scheme.

Ronald Hiscoke

WOODLAND FLOWERS

Under a canopy of green, carpets of bluebells stand erect.
Like rows of soldiers, side by side.
Their bell-shaped flowers cascading down.
As they shelter under towering trees.

Pale yellow primroses show their pretty heads.
Peeping out from rosettes of leaves.
Colourful clumps adorning mossy banks.
Their fragrance sweetening the damp Spring air.

Protected by a lush green jungle of leaves.
Fragile violets are hidden from view.
Weeping heads take you by surprise.
As their heavenly scent reveals where they hide.

Linda Ife

THE BEAUTY OF SPRING

Once the dark cloaks of Winter are shed.

The iridescent crocus peeps out from carpets of grass.
Kaleidoscopes of sweet scented polyanthus, brighten colourless
Flowerbeds.
Daffodils and their pretty, golden trumpet shaped heads.

Lush green leaves shimmer as they reflect the sun.
The once bare trees, form a canopy against a backdrop of cobalt
skies,
Shielding banks of pale yellow primroses from prying eyes.

Refreshing April showers swell infant buds, as they uncurl and
blossom Into maturity.
Pretty lambs play and skip in meadows damp with dew.
Wild birds flutter from mate to mate, ready to start life anew.

The beauty of Spring, is the beginning of life.

Linda Ife

SPOILED FOR CHOICE

Spoiled for choice just what do you do
If only it had amounted to just a few,
It makes the job so very hard
Really puts you on your guard.

What shall I buy just this or that
Or something cosy for my flat.
Cannot make up my mind it seems
I want the object of my dreams.

No, I decide, this is just not on
I will be unhappy when my moneys gone.
Well I suppose, I was just spoiled for choice
But I listened to my inner voice.

June Jackson

INNER CHILD

In the womb where life begins,
Mothers heartbeat, softly thumping,
Tiny baby safely sleeping,
Conflict and confusion, no place in this world.
Suddenly thrown in the depths of life,
Words are formed, personality emerges,
Into the playground, children laughing,
Discovering life through innocent eyes,
Teenage tantrums, confusion and rebellion,
Whole world turned upside down,
Adult emotions now in full swing,
I want to be a child again,
To look at life with simplicity and wonder,
To play on the swing, chattering idly,
Then deep from within, I hear a whisper,
'Go and play' it softly says 'retrieve your innocence'
Adult body, fully grown.
But forever holding on to the child inside,
My inner child.
The child I thought I had lost forever.

Michelle Jeffrey

OUTCAST

A vacant expression sits on her face,
Doesn't know what day or what year.
Huddled, freezing, nowhere to turn,
Eyes unseeing, not a sound does she hear.

No-one to love her, no-one to care,
Walking the streets, ignored and alone,
Society's outcast, shunned and despised,
Nowhere to run, no place to call home.

Begging for money, she says to buy food,
But up to the dealer, a need for release,
People want money, don't care of her fate,
But out of her mind, once more she finds peace.

The rain splatters down, but no notice she takes,
Soaking her clothes, drenching her skin,
Body trembling, lips turning blue,
Only sensation, the drug rushes in.

The cold light of dawn, a new day begins,
But for one lonely girl, the prospects are nil,
No more tomorrow's, no future to see,
Crouched in a doorway, her body lies still.

Michelle Jeffrey

HEAVEN

Is heaven the age before we are aware the maternal bliss?
Or the hug and cuddle of a mother or a sweet girl's caressing kiss?
Or is it raining over spring time hills jumping like lambs into the air
Or is it when we remember sentimental things and just stand and
stare.

Is heaven a beautiful kingdom somewhere up there in the sky?
The rest from the struggles of life, the eternity after we die?
Being away from home a long long time and finally coming home to
Stay
The joy of working on a farm, milking cows baying in the hay.

Is heaven a final achievement, we have worked for all life long?
Getting up early on a summers morn hearing birds sing beautiful
Songs.
For me it is the refreshment of a hot bath, my how we feel tingly and
Good.
Deciding whether we should go to that dance and deciding that we
Should.

Heaven for me was drinking of iced coke on a very hot day.
The building excitement the final climax of a very thrilling play.
The moment when my team breaks through scores, that winning
goal.
The flowing warmth and comfort in winter, from the heat of burning
Coal.

For me heaven is the acting out of positive ideas from a dynamic
Mind.
The beautiful lines of a lovely shape or unusual design.
It could be the carrying out of someone's last wish their dying desire.
The knowledge that you are on the way up and going higher and
Higher.

Heaven can be for the old as well as the young in age.
It could be the reading of a good book, the eagerness to read the next
Page.
Paradise is within you the Lord said as bread has the leaven.
Fight the good fight we call life, and I think you should know
heaven.

Richard Jones

ON THOMAS CHATTERTON

Gaze on my body, and know that I am dead
I lay lifeless, with not one thought in my head.
My body is at rest in such quiet repose
Nothing ever seems to be as we sometimes suppose.
In the spring of my youth, why did I not chose to live;
Tis final selfishness of mine who can ever forgive
Suicidal death this cruel world received from me.
The sacrificial lamb is what Thomas Chatterton chose to be
Misunderstood, by those of far lesser understanding
Unappreciated, it was my life-blood they were demanding.
Rejection poisoned me as nothing else ever could
This poet's heart is not made of stone, iron or wood.
Understand you this dead poet if you dare
That this poet's heart it was born to care.
That the Lord created poets to reflect His love and light
To show to this cruel world what is kind and right.
With His loving inspiration He binds us to ink and pen
To shed His light of love on this world of men.
They say of me 'he hast gone to Shakespeare'
'That wonderful boy,' with that soul so dear.
How that I died a sad and lonely death before my time
Death claiming me first then eternity saying he is all mine.
I say, what was lost one day will one day be found.
The door locked at night opens when morn comes round
A setting sun rises with the coming of dawn.
A rose reaches for the light with the coming of the morn;
Misunderstood, unappreciated, rejected did I do what was best,
Having gone to Shakespeare, the Lord will it, I will find my rest.

Richard Jones

WILD IMAGININGS

Imagination...use it well
For in wise use treasured peace
Does dwell.
Prune it like you would a bush
Chide it when it fails to hush.

Try discipline - imagination rises
In respect,
Show it who is master for, given free rein
It will ensnare you
And you'll never be master again.

Joy Lennick

BLATCHINGTON

Lord, what a day, what a beautiful day!!
Sweet smelling violets, Purple and white
Beneath the trees, hiding from the easterly winds.
Patches of dog violets blue as if the sky
Had fallen down and stayed on the grass.
Clusters of celandines like pots of gold
glow in the thick, rough grass.
The gorse, in places so thick with flower,
That no prickles could be seen.
And any moment now the blackthorn will burst
Forth in drifts of white blossom.

O Lord, what a wonder is Your creation
Seen on a splendid day in
Warm, warm sunshine, so welcomed
After the winter winds and grey days.
It was **good** to be alive today.

Mary-Joan Lloyd

HINDS' FEET

We are His
Chosen, before time
Called and called every day, every moment.
Sealed, stamped with His image
The stamp of ownership,
A guarantee,
Branded,
For God has established us
In Christ and commissioned us,
Giving us Holy Spirit in our hearts -
For we are His.

Wherefore we are content
In every condition -
In the valley or on the mountain top.
If we trust Him, He will lead us
To the high places.
Though the Way be strewn with rocks
Hard work, an uphill struggle,
He will give us hinds' feet
And a helping Hand,
To overcome all.

Mary-Joan Lloyd

THE CLOBBER INDUSTRY

Nee-nor-nee-nor-nee-nor.

The industry's retro-alarm
Signals a fashion emergency.
And a revival
Of your dad's youth.
(Only he's too old now
To appreciate it).

The old skool clobber,
Dragged from cob-webs,
Lofts and closets,
Is screaming.
It's bleeding
A forgotten colour
All over the recycle designers.

It begs on its knees,
'Somebody please,
Get me a tailor.'
So they rush it off to theatre.

The operation takes weeks
Of surgical alchemy. And
After needle anaesthetic wears,
It opens its eyes,
Re-born in disguise
As fresh clobber,
Nu clobber.
Old skool clobber
With interminable
Nobs on.

Nee-nor-nee-noe-nee-noe.

Marco

ZERO DE-NIRO BAR THE GIRO

Thursday is giro day, de-niro day,
Horse without the hay day.
I sign a form for my pay. And tell
The clerk I've done no work,
I've done no play.

Employers have sent me away,
I always say,
Though I beg, I plead, I pray.
My mind's starting to fray.
I'm running low on confidence-spray,
My ship's becalmed in a bay,
My blue skies are being
Re-decorated grey.

The clerk always nods at my dismay,
But her attentions soon stray,
As she puts my form
Back in its tray.
Then steers her eyes towards
Another,
Eager to sign on giro day.

Marco

RAINBOWS ON MY WALL

Sunlight filtering through the windows
Catch the edge of my mirror where,
In return it sends it prisms,
Of coloured lights into the air.
And on my wall, they gently land
As if painted, by a heavenly hand.

As I gazed into the garden
Watching the leaves as they softly fall,
I know that if I look behind,
I'll see God's rainbows on my wall.

Our lives drift by like falling leaves,
And we feel sad when summer's through,
But on the dullest, darkest day,
We can see His diamonds in the dew.

When I talk with my Dear Lord,
And ask forgiveness when I fall,
He gently turns me round to see,
My tears make rainbows, on His wall.

Marilyn Michaels

THE TREE OF LIFE

Life is a book of chapters three
The past, the present and yet to be.

The past has gone it is stowed away
The present we still live from day to day.

The future is not for us to see
It's locked away God holds the key.

The quiet one

THE RIVER

(For Brigid)

You wonder what I think of you,
When you stare into my eyes,
What thoughts swirl behind the blues,
Memories, plans or lies?

What are my thoughts, late at night,
When I lie upon my bed?
Do I sleep to the morning's light,
With visions of you in my head?

Or perhaps devious plans abound,
In the sea-scape of my dreams,
Without your anchor in waking ground,
Who knows what things I scheme?

Together only in instalments,
And loneliness takes its toll,
To flood your mind with a worried lament,
And doubts to plague the soul.

And what do I see in the future,
Do you sail with me in this unknown terrain?
And as time saps our souls like a blood-sucking creature,
Am I your savour or his partner in pain?

To give a certain answer,
When you ask of me these things,
Would be a greater fallacy,
Than any I could bring.

For like a twig in the river of time,
I take the course the current gives,
But in the moments that I find,
You're simply the one I want to be with.

Torsten Payne

A DREAM AWAY

Memories haunt my woken dreams,
As I lay me down to rest,
Your scent dresses the midnight air,
As your warmth caresses my chest.

And in the silver of the shadows,
I turn to hold you tight,
But the cool of the sheets reminds me,
As loneliness swallows the night.

And when the daylight breaks the dream of you,
I look to your pillow for the words upon it,
To read the script with a swollen heart,
That sounds to me as a perfect sonnet.

And my words have never seemed so humble,
So poor at saying what I feel is true,
But I try and hope you know my heart,
When I say I love and miss you.

Torsten Payne

THE DREAM

I dreamt I saw three angels
Standing by my bed
The first one looked at me and sighed
I trembled as he said:
'You have an extra mile to walk
Before your time is through
Prepare yourself to follow on
And do what you must do.'

The second angel smiled and said:
'Take heed of what we say
But first look deep within yourself
And you will find your way.'
The third one never said a word
But held a lamp so bright-
Then suddenly the lamp went out
And they disappeared from sight.

My dream was opportunity
My faith was strong and true
I stood by my achievements
But there was much more I could do.
So as I walk that extra mile
With options open wide
I'm sure that when my Master calls
He'll know at best I tried.

June Pledger

AUTUMN

The glories of autumn are with us,
The low sun is still full of warmth,
I wish I could share the wonders with you,
I wish you were here.

The garden is looking autumnal,
The lawn is untidy with leaves,
Flashes of colour appearing,
And I wish you were here.

The apples are nearly gathered,
The last few shine out on the tree,
The dogwood's leaves are rich ruby red,
I wish you were here.

The holly is heavy with berries,
Showing bright 'gainst the dark green leaves,
Food for the missels in winter,
I wish you were here.

Layered mist keeps the countryside hidden,
Which late sun has a struggle to clear,
Leaves dropping silently down to the ground,
And I wish you were here.

Gold, red and green in the garden,
In order as ever it was,
Cosy evenings are almost upon us,
But I wish you were here.

Margaret Francis Porter

A LIVING CAMERA

The minds a wonderful thing you know,
It stores many memories over the years as we grow.
Even the greatest camera in the world, taking pictures oh so well
Cannot take picture like one brain cell.
It snaps a memory and stores it there
For no one but you, it's time to share.
Good or bad it's stored within
It will always remind you of past gone sins.
Childhood memories stay there till you're old,
Teenage years when you were oh so bold.
A past love, a kiss in the dark.
Whilst strolling hand in hand through the park.
The grief for a loved one who's gone forever
But not in your head, they're there whatever.
So you see how wonderful the brain can be
Nothing can be taken away from me.

Amanda Potter

A VISIT

Do you ever get the feeling
That your never quite alone?
I don't mean evil spirits
That clunk their chains and groan..

I mean that eerie feeling,
Yet nothing really bad,
Just something, someone maybe,
You know, when you feel sad.

It's like they've paid a visit,
Because you miss them so,
Then suddenly the feelings gone
And you know they've had to go.

It's quite a comfort really,
To know they're still around,
It's the silence that's quite scary
Because they never make a sound.

Still, we should count our blessings
That they come down from up above,
They take the time to think of us,
And surround us with their love.

So whenever you feel lonely
And nothing seems worthwhile,
Just close your eyes a moment
- And they will bring a smile.

Gill Powell

REBEL

They said I was naughty,
When I was very young,
Always 'kinder' throwing things,
And chewing lots of gum.
Call me rebellious, swinging on my chair,
Always giving the teachers a fright,
And a rotten scare.
I didn't want to work, or
Comply to boring school;
Couldn't make much sense of it,
So I broke all the rules.
Teenage years were the worst,
Coming home late,
Waiting up was my Mum,
With an ill forfeiting fate.
Now I am a parent, I reflect with hindsight,
All the problems my parents had,
I thank GOD;
I've turned out alright.

Jill Preston

THANKS

You were the soul I never knew,
Yet you were there while I grew
From a babe to a child to an adult,
But now you can't share the result
Of your tender care and tuition
Still, call it intuition,
I know you're there, watching,
Willing me to achieve
The goals that you believed
Were mine by right; passed on
From Father to son.
So, while I grieve for the loss
Of my giver, my teacher, my soul master,
There is comfort in feeling you there,
And always my soul I can bear
To the spirit forever with me,
And, if I make a mistake, please forgive me,
Which I know you will, 'cause you cared
Enough to give life and love; you're spared
Any heartache I may bring
By forgetting your guidance and teaching;
But one day I'll make good and I'm glad
That I had you for my Dad.

Nigel Purssell

(For my Father - 26.7.O5 - 26.11.95 - R.I.P.)

STAR

Unique.
Like the curly locks on your head,
Or the radiance you bring into the room,
Touching people as you pass them by.

Like each new year,
Unique,
As one new number joins the existing digits.
One new friend has entered my life,
Never to leave in soul,
If in person,

As an angel lies in you,
Which has made mine wiser still.
But if you haven't found it yet my star,
Be sure, one day, you will.

Konce Ramadan

THE FEELING

Flow of music to my ears,
Entering the dark tunnel of love,
Deeper you push the feeling
So that after feeling the riveting climax,
I cannot come down, and yearn for more.

An ecstasy of breathing,
An orgasm of life
You bring me.
A gift that cannot be purchased,
Like a spirit cannot be held.

Lust shall never power
Over what I hold for you, in its
Very permeable case through which
Every drop of potion seeps, diffuses.

To capture your body, mind, heart, soul,
You.
Eternity love,
I shall be thine.
And smile.

Konce Ramadan

'FELLOW TENANTS'

The world in which we live, we simply do not own
The world in which we live, is simply just on loan
We complain and moan about its state
It's changing at a rapid rate
Realise now, before too late
It's man that is the villain

The world in which we live, we imply do not own
The world in which we live, is simply just on loan
We can't continue to pollute the air,
To fell the forests until they're bare.
To infect the waters without a care,
It's man that is the villain

The world in which we live, we simply do not own
The world in which we live, is simply just on loan
If just for all our children's sake
Then liberties we should not take
A concerted effort we all should make
To ensure that man is not the villain.

Nicki Rhodes-Foster

ONE SUMMER MORNING

As I rode through some busy streets,
To the nearby countryside,
Left behind were those sights and sounds
Replaced now by green fields wide;
Soon I entered a country lane
To a corner by a stream,
I stopped to sit and ponder,
In quietness to dream;
Ducks floated gracefully on their way,
Birds chirped their pleasant song,
Willow trees gently swayed in the breeze,
I could have stayed there all day long,
Soon however I had to return
Back to the noise and the grime,
Then Jesus words rang in my ear,
'To everything there is a time.'
So help me Lord to appreciate
That wherever I may be,
Each place has its contribution
In life's varied pattern for me
And I say 'THANK YOU LORD.'

Joan Riches

FRIENDS

Once upon a spring like day
When daffodils stand tall
I stand and listen - to my delight
I hear the bull frogs call.

The air is fresh the sun shines bright
Upon the waters still
The wind it blows the ears of corn
Outside the ancient Mill.

And as we run barefoot and free
Along the river bank
We leave behind the city life
As our minds feel light and blank.

I knew you'd be my true love
From the first time that we met
You helped to mend my broken heart
And things that hurt - forget.

The first time that I saw your face
I knew it was meant to be
Now that I had met you
You were mine for all to see.

You're always pleased to see me
You love to fool around
You sneak beneath my duvet
And never make a sound.

And when you came right home with me.
I could not believe my luck
For you are so very dear because
You are my precious Pup!

Anne E. Roberts

MYSELF

Every day I look at you
It makes me want to cry,
I now no longer know myself
So withdrawn and shy.

I'm not the one I used to be
But recognise the face,
I look into the mirror
The lines and crevasses I trace.

Where's the girl I used to know?
Ambitions bright and gay,
Somehow they all seem lost now
Forgotten gone away.

The eyes that once had danced like jewels
Look dull and lifeless now,
You'd like to stop your body clock
But just do not know how.

With nights filled full of anguish
The days seem that way too,
You can't remember happiness
You're always feeling blue.

The knocks in life can be so tough
It breaks a spirits heart,
You died from deep within yourself
Contentment never starts.

I wish someone would rescue me
I always feel upset,
To be the one I used to be
Not dragged down in life's net.

Anne E. Roberts

SALT OF THE EARTH

The daily news, constantly,
Reminds of man's inhumanity.
Very seldom do we hear
That every day, in every year
Kindly folk, find time to spare
To help others, in need of love and care.
Their names are known to just a few
And the value of the work they do
No price can be put on their worth
Thank You, '**Salt Of The Earth**'.

Ted Rogers

HAPPINESS

What of this life if full of stress
Affecting health and happiness,
Too concerned with materialistic wealth
Too much emphasis on self.
Impatient when someone who
May sometimes disagree with you,
Rushing here, rushing there,
No time to spare, no time to care,
No time to pause or slow down,
To let a smile, replace a frown.
Time to review, to think anew
What is happening to you,
Health is wealth, most would agree
Let happiness be your priority.

Ted Rogers

THE POET

The poet will strive to create
Word's of sensitivity,
To tell of wonders that abound
Of blessings God given free.
The purpose of our being
Stimulate our thoughts to dwell,
The wisdom of philosophy; our values,
The poetic verse will tell.
In the face of all aridity
Faith and hope shine through,
True love, sincere, eternal,
Poetry awakens past memories too.
'The pen is mightier than the sword'
All poets would agree,
And hope that their endeavours,
Help to enrich humanity.

Ted Rogers

JEALOUSY

The pain and the anguish
Brought on by this force
Is not natural or wanted
It's unfounded of course

Don't let it gnaw away
At your body and mind
Let out all your feelings
Be they cruel or kind

Clear your mind now
Close all the doors
Before this force ruins
The trust that was yours

This evil force creeps
Into every waking minute
Distorts out of focus
The evidence in it

Your confidence and pride
Being torn apart
Losing all control
Of head and heart

Take hold of this force
And stamp it out
Get back in control
Let it have no clout

If you feed this force
Give into the strife
You'll hate yourself
It'll take over your life.

Sharon Rosenwould

A DARKENED ROOM

Crouching in the corner while confusion causes fear
She sees herself in a reflection of her mother's tear.
And it makes her feel like dying.

Secrets playing with her mind.
There's no-one here to tell.
The loneliness is laughing
And it's lonely here in Hell.

There are painful scars on her body,
There is evil in her soul,
Her skin is thin and stretchy
And her spirit has dissolved.

You punched her starving stomach;
You had her on her knees,
You created all the secrets
And yet you're the one she needs.

Sabby

'TALKING TO YOURSELF'

Twisting thoughts and evil voices have their fun while you are asleep
They taunt you with threats to tell of the secrets that you keep.
Churning your mind with no thoughts or feeling
Laughing at what you are scared of revealing.

No image too gruesome,
They weaken your mind
'Til slowly you are falling,
Falling behind.

You try to close your eyes, but they are already waiting,
You try to run but your body's deflating.
The guilt is so great it's holding you back
And the voices are just waiting for their attack.

You bleed in their triumph
You cry when they win
Defeated and powerless
Is the state they leave you in.

You cannot escape from your own diseased mind
Your secrets will still be left to find
The voices will talk but you're too weak to listen -
No control, no hope and no ambition.

Sabby

AN ISLANDER

Born and bred on an island,
How it was formed, no clue.
Deep sky above, bright clear blue,
Could see nothing to feel blue.
Hears the gentle murmur of palm fronds,
Come from a community, united with family bonds.
Live in peace, safe and sound,
This is the simple life of an islander.
Not much expectations, to consider,
Except heavy breakers, breaking against the break-water.
No crimes, like robbery, cold-blooded killing,
Unheard of raping or street mugging.
Grew-up in an atmosphere of friendly feeling,
Free from evil thoughts, not concerned.
Their unspoilt minds are enlightened,
And engaged in daily work, whatever interested.

Ali Shareef

SAVE THE TURTLES

The sun sinking down on the horizon,
Light gently fades across the ocean.
Thunderous roar of the waves,
Crashing against the reef stone,
Sending misty clouds of spray.
While the new-born turtles under the sands,
Coming out and creeping on the beach.
Finding the shortest way with no one to teach,
To start an incredible journey out to sea.
Few of them survived, under the natural process,
But it brings no harm to the balance of species.
If the people are kind enough to them,
Need not put on the list of endangered.
What a wonderful, amphibious creature,
'Live and Let Live,' in order to complete the picture.

Ali Shareef

THE BIG BLACK CAT

The wind was blowing cold outside,
The sky was very black,
There upon the garden fence sits
The neighbours big black cat.

Underneath the huge conifer,
He sits so patiently,
I wonder what he's waiting for?
It's certainly not for me!

Off I trot to the shops,
And then I come straight back,
Sure enough upon the fence,
Still sits that big black cat.

Oh! I know what he's about!
He's after that white dove,
But he will be unlucky,
Cos he's cared for from above.

Gladys Sharp

THE FUTILE INSTRUMENT

Life is holding on by the barest of thread,
The apocalypse it rages on inside my broken head,
My eyes explode in burning balls of flame,
And I'm not quite sure just who to blame.

The bangs and the noise and the woeful screams of pain,
Shrapnel coming down all around like falling rain,
People running screaming, through the streets they go,
Why must this happen to us? Is all they want to know.

Burning shells of buildings are scattered all around,
But when the army marches on there's very little sound,
People lying sobbing, crying at their loss,
The dead then buried in mass graves with a solitary white cross.

In an ideal world there would be no use for guns,
All nations would unite, be friends, guns idle in the sun,
But the world we're in is not ideal, indeed a great shame,
And guns, and tanks and bombs are in use all the same.

People all the world throughout, they still are getting killed,
Surely now it's time for all the fighting to be stilled?

David Sheehan

THE VALLEY OF THE KINGS

To look in wonder on this place.
Treasures time cannot erase.
Most buried far beneath the sand.
This once glorious magnificent land.

From thousands of years before,
How many times did mourners pour.
To lie their kings in prepared tombs.
Placing his treasures in all the rooms.

All he would need in after life.
Even weapon in times of strife.
To the death mask most of gold.
What wondrous beauty to behold.

Their tombs they did not want disturbed.
Then we their names would not have heard.
Inscribed on tombs where kings have lain;
Speak of the dead and they live again.

Vanessa Sherwood

JUST ONE MORE

He sits alone and ponders on his wasted life,
Why did they all desert him, his kids his darling wife?
He knows full well what came between them was the demon drink,
It only started with a few, it helped to make him think.
As time went by the few got more, the more became a need,
Until it was the drink that ruled and his life was full of greed.

Self was now his main obsession he did not have a care,
As long as he was drinking it mattered not when or where.
Parties spending money friends he had them all
The devil had tomorrow but tonight he'd have a ball.
The nights were long his body knew that it was time to stop,
Tomorrow yes but just for now another pill he'd pop.

His wife and kids had had enough it's time for them to go,
He will never mend his ways she said he's not the man I know,
Now he sits alone at night around an open fire,
As he throws away his empty bottle this life will soon expire.

Tomorrow when his head is clear then things won't seem so bad,
He'll drink no more he'll clean himself and go back to what he had.
I must leave this place this dump I'm in the mire and the stench,
It's not a life to live no more so from it I must wrench.

With this thought he tells himself and that makes him smile,
The journey he is about to take is more than just a mile,
He pulls his coat around himself and shivers in the wind,
Staring into dancing flames he knows that he can find,
The life he lost he'll have again for he only had to think,
It's all so clear what he must do tomorrow,
But tonight my friends we'll drink.

William Singleton

THE OLD BUSKER

Old man in baggy trousers playing music not too loud,
People busy shopping dodging weaving in the crowd,
The man he sings a muffled tune and plays an old guitar,
A penny tossed from within the throng from his voice a crackled Ta!
He plays the songs of yesterday. No one can understand,
He plucks the strings with fingers bent from years working on the Land.

The guitar case lies on the floor it holds what folk can spare,
The old man hopes if he plays well he'll become a millionaire.
The market square is busy now as sellers sell their wares,
People rushing to and fro and no one really cares.
The old man sings his latest song the one to end the show,
Then he bends and picks his pennies up for he has somewhere else to Go.

The people do not notice as the old man takes his leave,
He will be back next market day on this you can believe,
It's sad to think the old man is alone but that's his choice,
Once around the corner. He is off in a big Rolls Royce.

William Singleton

ONCE THE TYGER!
(After William Blake's 'The Tyger')

Tyger! Tyger! burning bright,
Oh how awful is thy plight!
What destructive hand or eye
Has sworn thy race should die?

In what forests once so deep
Is thy very life now held so cheap?
Why this price upon thy head
That will not end till thou art dead?

And what bullet, and what gun
Will not kill thee though thou run?
And when all are slain but one
Wilt thou know the end has come?

What dire weapon, what dread arm
Will not kill or do thee harm?
And what hidden pit or iron snare
Will not snuff your life out there?

When Nature made thee fierce and proud
To roam the forests, thy head unbowed,
She could see the end that lay in store
Did she know thy kind might be no more?

Tyger! Tyger! burning once so bright,
I dare not think upon thy plight!
What destructive hand or lustful eye
Will cause one day thy race to die?

Christopher Stavrou

THE OLD HOUSE

The house stands empty now
Of all it once contained;
Of all the things that made it home,
Not one thing has remained.

And yet for me it's full of shadows
Of the life that went on there,
Of the people who called it home,
Of their hopes and their despair.

Tho' many years have now gone by,
I see it still so sharp, so clear,
It is as though I'm looking through
An open window onto yesteryear.

This is the place where I grew up,
My home and hearth for many years,
But now it shelters not a soul,
Nor hears the sound of joy or tears.

Soon the house itself will cease to be,
A motor-way will take its place,
And of the house that once stood here,
There will not be the slightest trace.

Proud it stands amidst the desolation
In a street condemned to disappear,
A stream of roaring traffic will replace
The home that many held so dear.

I exit through the doorless doorway
Back into the silent, lifeless street,
The stillness that now reigns there
Has never been so utterly complete.

Christopher Stavrou

WE CAME WE SAW WE LEFT

All walks of life, different people I have met,
I've had different mates,
Worked with different colleagues,
And other associates.

Hope I leave a lasting impression
On people I meet and see,
Some would have liked,
Others disliked me.

I've left my mark on this life,
There's been plenty of controversy,
But nowadays I just like to see,
People around me happy.

Hope I've touched the hearts,
Of loved ones and friends,
When you're on that final destination,
It's too late to make amends.

Does our spirit really leave our body
When we die? No one can tell.
Do we all go to heaven,
Or some condemned to hell?

On the other side do we meet up,
With old friends and family?
This thought gives us something
To hold onto, on our final journey.

A slab of marble to remind people,
That you were once there,
In the graveyards that's all that remains,
Do the living care?

My memory lives on hopefully,
Certain people will speak of me fondly,
It's a reassuring thought,
That comforts me.

We came, we saw, we left,
Hopefully, I've made some sort of effect,
I can rest in peace, knowing
I was likeable and gained respect.

Brian Stoneman

SHUT MY EYES

Lazy Sunday summer afternoon I lay here time is standing still.
One cloud just floating in a blue sky the mood is tranquil.
Not a care in the world the summer sun beating down on me.
In the distance you can hear the birds chatting in a tree,
My mind then starts to think about the world we live in,
Secret and private thoughts make me grin.
Then I think about people less fortunate and my grin disappears.
To end up disabled or terminal ill are my worst fears.

Blind people or the deaf and dumb who can't make a sound,
Disease and decay is all around.
People suffering with Cancer or Aids and what about the homeless?
Today's Britain couldn't care less.
Children born autistic or the mentally disabled,
Classed as vegetables are cruelly labelled.
Money and material things don't mean anything it puts it all into
Perspective
I'm one of the lucky ones in this life we live.

Like many others I shut my eyes to what's going on,
It don't concern me I know this attitude is wrong.
Family members rushing off to visit someone in hospital
somewhere,
To comfort them to show they care.
Surgeon somewhere making a life or death decision,
As he plunges in the scalpel with precise incision.
The only decision I have to make as I lay here,
Do I or do I not get up and get another cold beer.

Brian Stoneman

WHATEVER HAPPENED TO ONCE UPON A TIME?

Fairies in the garden
Dragons in the sky
Shadowy mists of Avalon
Risen high;
Home, some dark cave
In a far, distant time;
Poetry and heroes
Legends in their prime
Come to rescue us from
The terrors of bed-time;
All gone, kids grown
And who's passing on
Secrets of protection
To a generation
That prefers computer games
Or better still
Copy-cat storylines
From Pandora's Box?
(Issues of the day, strategy
In a ratings war, Peter Pan
Shot down over Walford)
New beasties
In the toy cupboard
Breaking out
Like chicken-pox
On a child's face
And no hiding place.

Roger N. Taber

NEW KIDS ON THE BLOCK

Gone shopping
Kids running wild
Trolley rage mums
All smiles;
Try the pub
Dogs everywhere
Kids shooting pool
Dads going spare;
On the pavement
Collide with some kid
On a bike (my fault
Forgot to look!)
Knives out in the playground
Acid in the park
Kids chasing death
For a lark;
Cops in their stride
Let's get even
Kids on a joyride
To heaven;
Mum's off her trolley
Dad's on the booze

Angel on the sideboard
Yesterday news

Roger N. Taber

CAVEMAN

In a damp gloom I wonder
Sometimes, stumble
Bang my head
On sudden stone
Hear a thrash
Of bats wings;
Though thoughts take flight
To a world that gloats
Above, like bats
They yearn, yearn
Returning,
Far, far into my soul
I grope for the truth
Of things, discover
Only history. (A gathering
Of bats in some
Remote cave!)
For now, I'll greet the sun
Embrace the wind, caress
Long grass, run wild
FREE - till, suddenly
Bats wings.

Roger N. Taber

TAKING IT EASY

The sounds of morning awakening as misty dawn steals away,
Reach my drowsy pillowed head, proclaiming another day.
The distant hum of traffic, the noise of a rushing train,
Planes winging their way to far off places, a new day begins again.

The gently whirr of the milk-float, bringing milk for our daily brew
Bantering voices of school-going children, the click of a high heel shoe.
The unmistakable sound of the dust-cart, the hurrying crew keeping Pace,
On the weekly collection of plastic bagged rubbish, less noisy than Those dustbin days.

Gates and vibrating letter-boxes herald the postman on his round,
Expectancy ends and I know he has passed when my gate and Letter-box make not a sound.
Car doors slamming, revving engines, screeching brakes all fill me With hate,
Drivers unbothered by their exhaust fumes, that through my fanlight Penetrate.

The pigeons up on my roof top will coo in vain for their daily bread,
For they know not I am taking my ease and spending the day in bed.
Thus another day begins, engulfed with comfort I lay,
Inertia holds me in a slothful-like grasp and I've no wish to break away.

Like a candle's allotted span, swiftly the hours decline, and dusk begins To settle in,
I know tomorrow if I'm spared, the daily routine will again begin.
It is an undisputed fact, nothing in this life comes free,
When I arise to face tomorrow, thrice busier I'll be.

Mary Tevlin

MR CAREY'S GROCERY SHOP

I remember oh so clearly when my mother would take me down,
To Mr. Carey's grocer shop, just outside our town.
A smiling face and courtesy, to my mother was extended,
Elegant in a tailored suit, for shopping she looked resplendent.
When pleasantries has been exchanged, across the counter tall,
I'd climb up onto a long legged chair, for I was then but small.
At her leisure my mother sat upon a comrade chair,
From which she gave her order, for a weekly bill of fare.
Mr. Carey would wink at me, and cuff me 'neath my chin,
Then reach up to the top-most shelf and bring down a large round
tin.
Off came the lid and I beheld, chocolates and toffees galore,
'Help yourself' such enticing words, 'til my mother said 'one no
more.'
As my face would fall she'd whisper, 'don't make a show of me,
Only one remember and say, thank you Mr. Carey.'
From golden mounds with wooden pats, such artistry be infused,
On a marble slab as he shaped and slapped and a pound of butter
Produced.
Nor did his skills lay at one door, no, Mr. C had many more,
Over large wooden chests (I see him now) his stout aproned figure
Would stoop,
From which he arose with tea or sugar in a metal scoop.
Then with admirable dexterity he'd weigh and pack would Mr.
Carey.
Sides of smoked bacon hanging aloft he reached with long-handled
Hook,
Patiently awaiting my mother's choice of cut, and a long long time
she Took,
The woody smoked carcass was then placed to lean, across the bacon
Slicing machine.
Biscuits were not packaged as they are today, in tilted tins with glass
Lids temptingly they lay.
Fresh eggs nestled in beds of straw, all sizes mixed together, some
With a cleavage of farm-yard, here and there a feather.

The days of instant coffee had not yet arrived, the better off drank
Percolated, others on Camp survived.
Fortress-like the counter stood between customer and shelves,
Temptation had no leaway as in these days of help yourselves.
When her shopping was complete, with cordiality, escorted to the
door We were by genial Mr. Carey.
Unburdened was my mother, empty handed as before, a messenger
Boy on a bicycle brought the shopping to our front door.

Here I stand in the present day, lining up to pay what is due, 'midst
Trolleys and boisterous children, a cog in a long long queue.
I think of my mother and Mr. C and those times that are no more, as
The faceless shoppers trundle wearily around that super store.
With three large bags of shopping I emerge through the revolving
door,
No messenger boy to unburden me, as in those courteous days of
yore.

Mary Tevlin

PUPPET ON A STRING

You twist me round your little paw,
Cos I love you so my dearest pet,
Do this, do that, feed me, open the door.
Your demands are many, but you change your mind,
Yet you hesitate and wait, half in, half out.
Make your mind up puss, we're losing the heat.
You dither, I'm getting cross, I want to scream and shout,
But with a gentle shove, I push you out.
Minutes later there's a thud at the door.
I look through the glass and what do I see?
You, you varmint! Come back for more.
I swear you do it just to torment me,
In the early hours you'll awaken me,
And worry till I let you out.
Think I'll do just that and throw away the key,
For you'll be back just when I'm dozing off
But though I rant and rave at you,
I'm a willing puppet on a string,
I wouldn't be without my boy so true,
Who on the doorstep waits so welcoming,
When I come home each day on cue.

Rose E.E. Thurley

AWAITING MINE HOST

Once ornate gates rust in disrepair
Long gone the people who once did care,
Flower beds choked by their own seeds,
Its gravel driveway like an ocean of weeds.
Ornamental bushes now distorted evergrown,
Surrounds this now rejected stately home,
The avenue of trees once erect full of grace
Take on a new image to match this place,
Their branches now twisted and deformed,
From things of beauty to horror transformed.
The houses paint-work peeling its woodwork bare
Rain stained windows like eyes of despair,
This building's heart and soul cries out in pain
Raped by the elements, the wind the rain.
Rusting fittings stain the carved oak door,
Dust and debris litter the floor
Dampen plaster falls from the walls
Portrays of passed owners adorn its hallowed halls.
The dining table set but in disarray,
A place where mice and spiders play,
Their beautiful webs hang heavy with dust,
The candelabras have lost their sheen, their lust,
Velvet drapes blackened by mildew
Dust giving this place a greyish hue,
And as darkening clouds drift across the night sky,
Reflecting the moons beams as they go by,
This along with the setting suns cold ray
Firing up the clouds at the end of its day,
With the silver of the moon and red and orange of the sun
Mixing of the elements with their course to run,
All awaiting the coming of mine host
The Lady in White and The Headless Ghost.

William Tremlett

EARTH'S HARVEST

In the dying embers of the harvest Sun,
Where wheaten fields are touched with gold
And the shadows lay long about the lane
In mellow contemplation,
The yielding earth displays its ripened riches
And the very World stands still.

In the crisp cold still of morning
Where the mist hangs heavy on the meadow
And the dew lays wet about the bough,
In a hushed expectant coming
The wakeful earth disrobes
And the very World stands still.

Philippa Trump

SPIRIT OF LOVE AND PEACE

Spirit of love and peace
Anointing One, divine,
O, breathe assurance to my soul
That I shall know Thee mine.

So would I look to Thee
O, hold me by Thy light
That darkened thought shall have no power
To stay me from Thy sight.

For when I'm cleansed from sin
By Jesus' precious blood
Then nought shall lure me from His way
As blessings o'er me flood.

And so I turn to Thee,
Spirit of love and peace,
To Thee - where separation ends
And tears forever cease.

Alan Rees Turner

MY OLD CARDBOARD BOX

There's a cardboard box in my closet
That bears the dust of time
It holds my childhood memories
Of the time when you were mine.

A box of infinite memories
A box of dreams and joy
Times of you as a young girl
And me when I was a boy.

It holds all your old love letters
I read then when I am blue
And think of things that might have been
Had I been true to you.

Leslie Velvin

A KISS SAYS IT ALL

As a Rose so tenderly administered,
Tears slowly trickle, then fall.
Hearts entwined, filled with emotion,
A kiss says it all.

One hand clasped tightly in two others
A penetrating gaze to hold,
A smile so warmly distributed
Will forgive the one so bold.

A contented sigh will go unnoticed
When the dusk begins to fall,
Hearts entwined, filled with emotion,
A kiss says it all.

Holli Wells

HIS LOVE

When all around you falls apart
And sadness fills a broken heart
His love can help to take away
The pain that haunts you night and day.

When something that you see or feel
Reminds you of so much to heal
His love can know your wounds so sore
He has the key to life and more.

It seems that life can never be
A joy to live again, to see
Happy faces, contentment true,
But He knows the hurt you're going through.

He lives in flowers, animals, a dove
This isn't the end - its just the start
If you give Him your broken heart.

Josephine Western

HOLIDAY THOUGHTS

My annual holiday is looming, they say it's good to get away.
To pack a case, lock up the house, and seek somewhere to stay.

I've searched through all the brochures, the ones abroad look grand.
With swimming pools, and posh hotels, and miles of golden sand.

The flight will cause no anxieties, people do it every day.
I'll be as safe as houses, especially once I pray.

Of course the languages different, but I'm sure they'll understand.
When I ask for my baked beans, with that special brand.

They say the beaches are crowded, but I'm sure to find a space.
I'll even get up early, to join in the morning race.

The tropical sun won't harm me, I'll take precautions not to burn.
I'll reserve an umbrella, if unlucky, wait my turn.

I'm told the swimming pools are inviting, full of people having fun
But then I'm not a mixer, I'll just wait until their gone.

In the evenings I'll go walking, the night clubs I don't desire.
Then back to sleep in my hotel, I hope I don't perspire.

The food of course is different, but I've eaten exotic meals.
I've even had an upset stomach, I know just how it feels.

They say that mosquito's can bite you, especially while you sleep.
But I'll take lots of special cream, and rub it in real deep.

My money will need changing, for some francs or even lira.
I do hope the new exchange rate, won't make it any dearer.

Well, I studied all the brochures, and considered where to roam.
But with all the possible drawbacks, I think I'll stay at home.

Roy Weston

INSOMNIA

Have you ever lain awake,
A restless prey to thought,
Worrying about those little things
That will probably come to nought.

Yet another weary glance
At the clock - face by the bed.
Just ten minutes have gone by
Since I looked at those hands of lead.

With eyes that feel like organ-stops,
I vow to think no more.
No sympathy from him who says
'You snored the night before.'

With the cold grey light of dawn,
I wonder, with a curse
What **did** I think about all night,
It must have been this verse!

Kathleen Westwood

TO A TERRORIST

You don't even know me,
We have never met.
Yet you decide that I must die
For the justice you want to get.

Here are my children
They're aged six and three.
Pretty girls, full of life.
You'd kill them to be free.

You'd allow us all to die,
Because you say you're right.
What can I do to stop you?
Nothing...my life is for your fight.

I may live or I may die,
You neither know nor care.
I have no voice in this fight,
I'm caught in your brutal snare.

An average family died today,
'Til now they were unknown.
Now a nation mourns their loss,
They bled to free your own.

Now I'll tidy up the dolls,
Put videos away.
Tuck the children up in their beds.
Pray violence never comes our way.

Jane Whittington

WHEN I WAS YOUNG

When winter's dirge the chimney filled, and I made toast,
The oven baking fruit-filled cake, my mother's Host;
I knew why ancients worshipped fire, with harp and lyre.

In summer fields of living green wove patterns gay,
And rippling streams and osier beds fringed fields of hay,
Or kingcups bold and iris yellow splashed the meadow.

Weekly the horse-drawn carrier's cart trundled to town,
Knee to knee the rustics yarned, parcels put down,
Beguiling time with rural wit and choice tit-bit.

At church they taught the golden rule - a new dimension;
We honoured it on field of play, or got detention.
We aped the man at home, at school - we played the fool!

Our world was small, land, sea and sky teased our cloisters;
Beyond, above, the stars would peep at we oysters;
Only in books we travelled far to glimpse our star.

Too soon the swiftly mounting years tight-laced the child,
Boldly the youth in the green tree chained passions wild,
Till he attained maturity - a pot-pourri.

Now, cows are milked in roundabouts, men leap the moon;
Nations contend by satellites - by drunken rune:
The rustics in the carrier's cart rode heart to heart.

Rev. J.S. Wilkinson

VANISHING

Vanishing. Like delicate petals of a rose
Trampled by a breathless autumn fall.
No rose is left for now it snows
And with it arrives winter's squall.
Vanishing. Like falling feathers on a stream
Gently drifting out of sight.
Floating away like loves lost dream
Sailing on into the distant night.
Vanishing. Like early spring's waking mist
Submitting to summer's morning glory.
No time is wasted through being kissed
By the falling autumn story.
Like the first signs of glistening dew,
The words of this sonnet are vanishing too.

Anthony Williams

THE MIRACLE

When a butterfly begins
It has no colour, it has no wings.
It hasn't even got a leg
Because it's just a tiny egg.

A caterpillar hatches out
And feeds upon the leaves of plants,
When fully grown its skin it sheds
And so becomes a chrysalis.

For some long time the chrysalis sleeps,
Until one day a change,
A butterfly emerges
Feeling somewhat strange.

It sits a while, then spreads its wings
And flies off from the ground,
It has to search for nectar
From the flowers all around .

Just one of Nature's Miracles
And such a dainty thing.
The butterfly so colourful
Can so much pleasure bring.

Pam Williams

AUTUMN'S PARTIES

Autumn is a singer
With many songs to sing
Songs of summer-days that have passed
Summer's farewell she brings.
The sun provides the lighting
For the Chestnut, Oak and Maple trees
To have an open air party
And dance with the winds gentle breeze.
The red, bronze and golden leaves
Swirl and dance around on the ground
Autumn watches happily
Enjoying the musical sound.
Autumn is a singer
With many songs to sing
She sings of all the happiness
Her parties always seem to bring.

Sheryl Williamson

AS I JOURNEY HOME AGAIN

How I love the world
On rainy nights,
When street lamps give off
Magical lights.

Making rain made pools shimmer,
On roads dark and sparkling like jet;
I could just sit and watch for hours,
As everything gets wet.

Each rainy pool reflects picture stories,
From all that's happening around.
They are projections of moving pictures,
Images devoid of sound.

In the countryside, leaves and stone walls
Seen special once made wet and surveyed at night
As street lamps shine on them;
They look especially glossy, colourful and bright.

On the sea shore,
Little difference from the norm, can be seen.
The huge rocks and cliffs that are always sprayed wet;
Still appear menacing and mean.

Sand castles, have long since
Been washed away.
Made by happy, playful children
Earlier in the day.

I see all these things through a window,
As I travel home on a train.
I hope it rains again tomorrow,
As I journey home this way again.

Sheryl Williamson

WORDS

So many words are written.
Why can't they be enough?
Why do I feel cheated?
Where can I find the truth?
My hunger is great!
How can words fill me up?
I'm surrounded by words
But they don't fill the gap.
My books were my all
My comfort and food,
Now I must starve
While still being wooed.
The words belong to others,
They are not mine alone,
They are others' thoughts and emotions
Now just turned to stone.
My mind is filled with words
Struggling for release,
They pour down through my pen,
Deaf to all my pleas.
How can I stem the flow
Of what the words will say?
My hand can write no faster,
But how can I tell it 'stay?'
I'm starved for a voice
That can tell how I feel.
But the words on the paper
Tell me I'm real.

Shirley Woodbridge

THE PAINTER

The road is long and hard
I paint its life.
The colours in my head fly down my arm, and through the brush
onto The canvas.
Life is here, all around me, yet distant from my soul
It plagues me. It will not let me be.
I cannot be a part of it, nor yet apart from it.
It wears me down.
I carry the hurts of the world. They fly at me like arrows, pinning me
To the earth.
Burning suns and midnight stars -
Dark passions of my mind.

Shirley Woodbridge

AS THINGS USED TO BE

As children we did dance
Around a may tree, light of heart,
As we grow older
The pleasures we see
Are the trees in blossom
Maple, Hawthorn and Cherry.
The first flush of Roses
Have yet to come,
Followed by Dahlias
In the hot July sun.
August a month of pure delight,
A profusion of colours, what a sight!
All too soon winter is here,
The sun might shine
It could be grey,
The wind could blow, as well it may,
Whatever befalls, have a nice day.

Sheila Woods